The Colour of Bondi

Rex Dupain

New Holland Publishers

Foreword
Sebastian Smee

You can see why good photographers are attracted to beaches. Only at the beach do the most private, intimate acts – acts that can be cherishably awkward one minute, stunningly sensual the next – take place in a public setting, under the full glare of the sun. And only at the beach do these intimate, unself-conscious acts coexist with so many deliberate, self-enjoying acts of physical display.

Degas had to hang around furtively backstage at the ballet to find a similar combination of theatrical display and oblivious down-time. At the modern-day beach, by contrast, there are no cramped rehearsal rooms or key holes to peer through: it's all out in the open, there for the taking.

The photographs in this book were taken by Rex Dupain at Bondi Beach between 2003 and 2006. They rise above postcard cliché thanks to the visual intelligence behind them and Dupain's special sensibility – classical, but not aloof; sensuous, but equally interested in characters, relationships, stories; candid, but not falsely dramatised.

Bondi is a visual feast, almost embarrassing in its amplitude. "It must be the corniest landscape ever recorded," says Dupain, "but guess what? It still moves everybody." It has a sort of ineradicable beauty. "Despite its mediocrity," the author of a local council planning proposal once wrote, Bondi "prevails. This is based entirely on the natural amenity of the beach. Man has contributed little."

It's true that, seen through the wrong lens, Bondi can look like a tourist-trap, a tacky commercial strip, even a rubbish tip. But its less immediately attractive qualities have a way of being rolled into the overall seduction, like retreating water into the sparkle and froth of waves crashing on sand. The ice-cream coloured architecture, for instance, all blockish and bedraggled, starts to look almost touching as it huddles on the thin wafer of sloping sand between sky and sea. The tourists, too, add to the beach's poetry of transience. And of course the beach itself, its sheer expanse, its inexhaustible, slaying sensuality, mesmerises.

To go to Bondi and not to interest oneself in all this would be to deny nature. But Rex Dupain presents us with something more than his own subjective interest. He finds images that hone and sharpen our own interest. His work, which is never staged or contrived, has a quality of objective alertness. "How interesting it is," he says, "to watch people do what they do, when they do it."

The camera is perfectly suited to capturing the beach's particular poetry. It's a poetry of transience, since at the beach everything is constantly changing: the weather, the water, the people, their states of dress. But it's not a rarefied poetry: it's a kind of joyous, democratic, light verse, a truly vernacular poetry, steeped in humour and poignancy.

"It is about timing, light and what the pictorial dice of the moment offers," says Dupain. "The strangest combination can occur when taking candid photographs. Uncanny resemblances to the classic myths and stories can take place without you asking permission."

An upside-down Russian muscleman, held from behind, takes on overtones of Titian's *The Flaying of Marsyus*. A beautiful woman showering herself with oblivious self-absorption reminds us of Diana at her bath, the voyeur behind her transformed into a stag with metal antlers. A man facing out to sea as a wave hits the wall of the pool and crashes over him is an exemplar of abandoned, hedonistic romanticism: Casper David Friedrich meets Hockney's *A Bigger Splash*.

Several things strike me as I leaf through these photographs. One is the lovely balance Dupain strikes between near and far — between the intimacy of a face and the pattern of a crowd; between the weight and proximity of two lovers in a clinch and the imperious calm of distant, brooding clouds.

The other is Dupain's feeling for colour. For most of his career, Dupain has worked in black-and-white. These images are a departure, and a welcome one, for it turns out that he is a brilliant colourist. "The simmer of water from headland to headland melts from turquoise to French ultramarine," he says. Blues of every hue form a kind of base note in the majority of these photos against which Dupain tunes carefully rationed outbreaks of other colours — sometimes bright and saturated (the girl in a pink cardigan with a pink hoop); at other times more subtle (the pastel yellow exterior, mostly in shadow, of a block of flats).

One of the book's masterpieces in this sense is *Contact*, which shows from behind a young couple on a metal bench looking out to sea. The water and sky are both in shades of blue, as are the couple's clothes. Surreally, the girl's legs are invisible (presumably jack-knifed up under her on the bench), but her rich russet hair hangs straight down over the back of the bench. It chimes delicately — so delicately that you don't notice it at first — with the rusty red of the bricks below and the pink of the boy's heel.

It's a superb image — not only in formal terms, but in human terms, too: what an amazing expression of ambivalent intimacy the girl's out-stretched arm is!

"On a good day," says Dupain, "the endless frustrations of the captured moment or non-captured moment rate at about 10 to 1, i.e. one captured moment to nine missed moments." And yet the rewards are generous. There are photographs here that could only have resulted from a perfect combination of patience, alertness and serendipity. *Shangri-La*, for instance, shows an old man walking along dragging his towel, like a captured soldier, or a morose Christopher Robin dragging Pooh homeward. The backdrop to his grizzled frame is a blonde block of flats ("SHANGRI-LA") with two brown doors, each one emblazoned with a white graphic of yachts in full sail. It's an image that combines dejection and bloom, stark artifice and grizzled reality. And it's very witty.

Occasionally, conscious of the inherent aesthetic appeal of his setting, Dupain plays havoc with our assumptions about what is real and what is artificial. There are, for instance, several photographs where he uses artificial backdrops — a peeling mural, say — to set off or make mischief with a posed subject's vivid reality. Likewise, in *Man with a Pram*, the yellow "sun" on the child's towel seems to have slipped a few inches from its rightful position in the picture-book blue sky.

Dupain shows us every aspect of Bondi and gives us glimpses of all the various subcultures that distinguish the place. The skaters at The Bowl, the musclemen at the outdoor gym, the backpackers, the divers, the young dads and mums, the surf lifesavers and the nippers, the swimmers and the surfers of every age, the Jews, the Japanese, the Lebanese, the lovers.

"To have no ego at all, just to be with the subjects and the subjects to be with you, is the smoothest way to shoot," he says. "We are all one." This would have to be the first chapter of Zen and the art of photography.

Bondi can be corny and it can be kitsch, as Dupain is the first to point out. But, he adds, "I think it's what Kenneth Slessor would say: 'you think it's ugly, I think it's lovely'."

Sebastian Smee
August 2006

Sebastian Smee is the national art critic for *The Australian*. He is the author of *Side by Side: Picasso v Matisse* and two books on the English painter Lucian Freud.

To my mother, Diana, whose love for people, nature and art will always inspire.

The Colour of Bondi

Rex Dupain

Portrait with Boards   2004

Surfer In the Sea   2003

Circle in the Sea   2003

Two Boards   2004

Little Nipper   2004

Couple in the Sea   2003

Piggy Back 2004

Standing in the Sea   2003

At the Carnival   2004

Lifesavers 2006

At the Start   2004

Bondi vs Maroubra   2006

Nippers with Boards   2004

Surf School   2005

Lifesavers with Oars   2006

The Big Heave   2006

Six Surfers   2005

Little Girl with Towel   2005

Bondi Transport   2006

Big Wave   2005

Lifesavers at Boat Race   2006

Figures in Surf 2004

Boat Crew   2006

Rolled   2006

Sea Edge   2003

Lifesaver   2006

Girl at Carnival   2006

Girls at Carnival   2006

Lifesavers at Carnival   2006

At the Gym   2005

Surf Boat in Haze   2006

Figures in Landscape   2005

Towel over Lifesaver   2006

The Frisbee   2003

By the Phone Booths   2006

Last of the Crew   2005

Surf Race 2004

Surf Patrol   2005

Line of Swimmers   2006

Skater   2006

Handstand   2005

Two Skaters   2004

Bike at Skate Ramp   2004

At the Skate Ramp   2004

In the Bowl 2006

The Black Hat   2006

Couple with White Surfboard   2006

Skate Ramp Scene   2006

Bondi Sleep   2006

Afternoon at the Bowl   2005

Man with Towel 2006

Three Bathers   2005

Bondi Girl   2006

Bondi Passover 2006

Bondi Venus   2005

Girl by the Boat   2005

The Paper Brolly 2006

Tourists 2006

Couple with Boards   2004

The Standover   2004

69

Sand Race   2005

Girl with Umbrella   2005

On the Sofa 2006

The Musician   2005

Pram on Sand   2005

Beauty and the Beast   2006

On the Rock   2006

Girl with Red Towel   2005

Bondi Rain   2005

Beach Scene 2004

Beach Scene with Yellow Board   2004

No Worries   2006

Under the Towel   2005

Contact 2005

Hug   2006

At the Beach 2006

Two Surfers   2006

Bondi Catwalk　2006

On the Beach 2006

Landscape with Carpark   2005

On the Kombi 2005

Seated Women 2006

Goal over Horizon   2006

Wet Day   2005

Bondi Torso   2006

Peak Hour   2005

A Memory   2005

Three Girls   2006

Women with Scarves   2005

Figures on the Sand   2005

Blonde Man   2006

Beach Scene with Umbrella   2006

Girl with Towel   2006

One Bodyboard   2005

The Fisherman   2005

Flags 2003

Splash Man   2006

High Tide   2005

Farewell My Lovely   2005

Winter on the Sand   2003

Surf and Rocks   2006

Boxers 2005

Man with Dogs 2006

Off the Rock   2005

Bathers in Landscape   2006

The Dad 2006

Bondi Family   2005

Girl with Scooter   2006

Landscape with Lambretta   2006

Fellows in Surf   2005

Old Lady 2006

By the Pavilion   2005

The Sundeck   2005

Man With Pram   2006

Landscape with Tents   2005

Family in the Wind   2006

Bondi Camouflage   2005

The Pink Cap   2005

Bondi Landscape   2006

Landscape with Surfer   2006

Coming Storm   2005

The Last Rays   2006

Over the Bridge   2005

Shangri-la   2005

Any Day   2004

Walking Cyclist   2006

Couple and Old Man   2005

Storm Clouds   2004

Dusk 2005

Interaction   2003

Double Rainbow   2005

From the Icebergs   2005

Walking Man at Sunset   2006

Two Girls Asleep   2006

Waters Edge at Dusk   2006

Girl with Hoop   2005

Beach Haven   2005

Red Board at Dusk   2004

Figure with Bodyboard   2005

Shadows over Torso   2006

Summer Rain   2005

Afternoon Jogger   2005

Lovers and Dog   2005

The Wetsuit   2005

Afternoon Landscape 2004

Dark Clouds   2004

Moonrise 2005

Last Light 2005

Out of the Sea 2005

Architectural Puddle   2005

First published in Australia in 2006 by
New Holland Publishers (Australia) Pty Ltd
Sydney • Auckland • London • Cape Town

14 Aquatic Drive Frenchs Forest NSW 2086 Australia
218 Lake Road Northcote Auckland New Zealand
86 Edgware Road London W2 2EA United Kingdom
80 McKenzie Street Cape Town 8001 South Africa

Copyright © 2006 in photographs: Rex Dupain
Copyright © 2006 New Holland Publishers (Australia) Pty Ltd

All rights reserved. No part of this publication may be reproduced, stored in a retrieval system or transmitted, in any form or by any means, electronic, mechanical, photocopying, recording or otherwise, without the prior written permission of the publishers and copyright holders.

Dupain, Rex, 1954- .
        The colour of Bondi.

        ISBN 1 74110 521 8 (hbk).
        ISBN 978-1-74110-521-6

        1. Beaches - New South Wales - Bondi - Pictorial works. 2.
        Photography, Artistic. 3. Bondi Beach (N.S.W.) - Pictorial
        works. I. Title.

        779.4099441

10 9 8 7 6 5 4 3 2 1

Publisher: Martin Ford
Designer: Greg Lamont
Production: Monique Layt
Reproduction: Pixel Perfect Pro Lab Pty Ltd
Printer: C&C Offset Printing Co